Quilts With Unique
BORDERS™
Extraordinary Border Finishes

Edited by Carolyn S. Vagts

Annie's®

Introduction

Take an ordinary quilt and make it extraordinary.

Not every quilt is all about the pieced blocks within. Sometimes a simple block setting is complemented by a fabulous border. Sometimes the border makes the quilt. *Quilts With Unique Borders* will give you options for stunning quilts with unique borders and the skills to make them. Don't be limited by conventional piecing construction. Think outside the box! Maybe what you're looking for is border accent options.

Blocks incorporated into a border, or combining borders to extend the length or size needn't be plain. With a little imagination borders can be the focal point of the quilt. Have you ever thought about adding a faux bargello border or creating a unique pattern rhythm? *Quilts With Unique Borders* has nine projects, all with uniquely different borders. These patterns will inspire you to take another look at an important design element that is often overlooked. Whether you choose to incorporate blocks in the borders or simply rethink how you make them and what you use as borders, you'll find exciting possibilities in *Quilts With Unique Borders*. Turn an otherwise ordinary quilt into an extraordinary work of art.

Table of Contents

Hexie Festoon,
page 19

Creating Extraordinary Borders

Most of us agree that there are five elements to a quilt top: blocks, setting squares or triangles, sashing, borders and bindings. All five elements add their own special touch to a quilt's overall design. But borders provide us with a secondary design opportunity while serving the very ordinary purpose of providing a frame for the quilt center and a way to easily enlarge the quilt.

A painter considers the frame for a completed masterpiece with as much care as was taken in planning the painting itself. The same should be true of borders for quilts.

Proportion

To avoid making the quilt center look out of proportion, match the border width to the size of the finished quilt. You should aim for a pleasing scale between the border width and the rest of the quilt's components. As a general rule of thumb plan your borders around the block sizes. Border size is a personal choice and may vary with each quilt. Explore all your options. If your blocks are 4" finished, start with a 4"-wide border, then try other border measurements. Each quilt is different, and there isn't a set rule for border size.

The border area can help expand the overall size of the quilt without multiplying the number of blocks or other elements. But don't just expand the width of the border. A too-wide border can make the quilt center design look small and out of proportion. Increase the border area width by adding multiple borders the same size or smaller than the blocks in the design.

Fall Splendor border.

Used as an edge treatment for a smaller quilt, like wall quilts, it may be worth more time and attention to create a border that provides a precise, but not necessarily wide, visual separation between the center focal point and its surroundings. Remember, however, that a too-narrow border can make the quilt center appear out of balance.

Basic Border Configurations & Calculations

There are three basic border configurations: straight, straight with mitered corners and straight with corner squares. Whether these borders are plain or decorative you will determine border widths and lengths needed in the same manner.

It is suggested that you cut borders on the lengthwise grain if possible. The lengthwise grain is more stable than the crosswise grain and less likely to stretch. Use the longest border to be cut to figure the yardage needed.

Seamless border lengths can often be justified when other patchwork, inner borders, etc., will be cut from one fabric. Estimate yardage with the full length of the borders cut along one edge of the fabric; other shapes can be cut from the remaining fabric width.

If cutting border yardage on the crosswise grain, add the total length of the borders and divide by the width of your fabric to calculate how many strips you will need to cut. Multiply the number of strips by the unfinished width of the border to calculate the yardage needed for your borders.

Begin by measuring vertically and horizontally through the center of the quilt, including seam allowances. These basic measurements will be the basis of all your border planning.

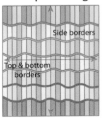

Measuring for Border Lengths

For straight borders, cut two lengths the border width indicated by the vertical length measured for side borders.

Cut two lengths the border width indicated by the horizontal length measured plus two times the unfinished border width; subtract 1" for seam allowances for top/bottom borders.

For straight borders with corner squares, cut two side borders the horizontal measurement and a top and bottom border the vertical measurement.

To calculate the length needed for corner squares, multiply the width of the unfinished border by four. Cut a strip the border width indicated by the calculated length. Subcut four squares for corners.

Corner squares will be stitched to the top or bottom borders before the borders are attached to the quilt top.

For straight borders with mitered corners, measure vertically and horizontally through the center of the quilt, including seam allowances.

For side and top/bottom borders, add twice the finished width of the border plus 2" for seam allowances to the horizontal or vertical measurements.

Beyond the Basic Border

Planning borders can be as simple as deciding color and width. But why stop there?

Plain borders can become pieced, appliquéd directional or dimensional borders using the straight, corner square or mitered corner treatments to complement both the border treatment and quilt center. The ideas and patterns in this book show how the border area can become a secondary design palette for the quilt designer.

Patchwork blocks can be the perfect complement to a simple patchwork center panel. Choose block designs that add an extra punch to a plain center design but still remain simple. The real challenge may be to get the border design elements to repeat pleasingly along the center panel edges.

Adding sashing or narrow pieced blocks between larger pieced blocks can solve any repeat problems. Using corner squares to keep a directional block in the correct orientation gives the repeat a smoother look.

Housing Boom border.

In Housing Boom on page 14, the pieced house blocks surround the checkerboard center like houses around a town square. To make the houses repeat pleasingly, tree sash strips were added and the corners repeat the checkerboard pattern of the center so that the houses all face the center.

A plain border between the center panel and a pieced border provides an area to allow for the difference between the block size and the size of the incremental border motif repeats.

In Classic Elegance Bed Runner on page 11, the quilt center is enlarged by using additional narrow plain borders added between the elements of the quilt center. The quilt center is then surrounded by courthouse steps blocks, and then finally a second narrow plain border.

Classic Elegance Bed Runner border.

Pieced borders within a quilt's layout, as well as near the edge, can be visually exciting and fun to create. However, the multiple seams can make the edges seem to lengthen or shrink on their own. A plain border can assist in confining the patchwork edge to its real, drafted size, providing a way to gauge where the patchwork intersections should fit, and to ease in any extra length in a manageable way.

Blushing Stars border.

Appliqué can be easily added to straight, straight-with-mitered corners or straight-with-corner squares borders. Appliqué can be resized or other appliqué elements like vines or leaves can be used to adjust the proportion of the appliqué to fit the border area while still carrying out the appliqué design.

Hexie Festoon border.

Directional borders pull the eye toward the center of the quilt or make it travel around the quilt edge by repeating a center design movement. These borders may take more planning to be sure that the border lengths can be adjusted to fit the quilt center and still keep the direction or movement repeating smoothly. The addition of corner squares or sashing may be required.

Dimension can be achieved by adding elements like appliquéd yo-yos or stitched in 3-D pieces such as the scallop shapes used on the Lots Dots quilt.

Lotsa Dots border.

Mitered corners add a formal appearance to any quilt especially when used in multiples of straight borders on either side of pieced borders. The mitered corner should be stitched accurately to lie flat so it works best on borders that are not pieced.

Checkerboard Beauty border.

Most piecing and appliqué techniques can be translated to the border area of your quilt to complement or expand the design of the quilt. Pay attention to proportion, border lengths and how your unique border will complete your quilt. Experiment with something new and complete your quilt with a memorable frame. ∎

Fall Splendor

Designed & Quilted by Julie Weaver

Bring the vibrant colors of fall to your walls—or a friend's—with this lovely wall quilt using a simple border technique to incorporate all your scraps for an extraordinary finish.

Specifications

Skill Level: Confident Beginner
Quilt Size: 36" x 36"

Materials

- 6" x 8" scrap each brown and 3 red/rust batiks
- 1 fat eighth green batik
- ⅔ yard cream batik
- 1⅛ yards brown batik
- 1⅛ yards total assorted autumn-color batiks
- Backing to size
- Batting to size
- Thread
- ¾ yard 18"-wide double-stick fusible web
- Template material
- Basic sewing tools and supplies

Cutting

Prepare templates for appliqué shapes using patterns given on the pattern insert. Cut as directed on patterns and in the instructions. Refer to Needle-Turn Appliqué on page 24 for alternate construction and cutting methods.

From cream batik:
- Cut 1 (18½" by fabric width) strip.
  Subcut strip into 1 (18½") A square.

From brown batik:
- Cut 10 (1½" by fabric width) strips.
  Subcut strips into 2 each strips as follows:
    1½" x 18½" B, 1½" x 20½" C , 1½" x 23½" F,
    1½" x 25½" G, 1½" x 30½" J and 1½" x 32½" K.
- Cut 1 (3" by fabric width) strip.
  Subcut strip into 4 each squares as follows:
    3" I, 2½" M and 2" E.
- Cut 4 (2¼" by fabric width) binding strips.

From autumn-color batiks:
- Cut 16 (2" x 5½") D rectangles.
- Cut 20 (3" x 5½") H rectangles.
- Cut 24 (2½" x 6") L rectangles.

Completing the Appliquéd Center

1. Trace appliqué shapes given onto one paper side of the fusible web, leaving space between pieces and referring to manufacturer's instructions and patterns for number to cut. Draw three ⅜" x 8½" stem shapes onto the paper side.

2. Cut out shapes, leaving a margin around each one; remove one paper liner. Stick shapes to the wrong side of fabrics as directed on patterns for color; stick the ⅜" x 8½" stem pieces onto the wrong side of the green batik. Lightly fuse shapes to fabrics.

3. Cut out shapes on traced lines; remove second paper liner.

4. Fold A and crease to mark the vertical and horizontal centers as shown in Figure 1.

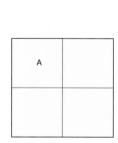

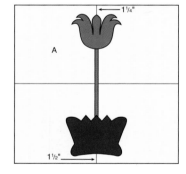

Figure 1   **Figure 2**

5. Center the plant pot 1½" from the bottom of A; temporarily stick in place. Center a stem and one flower above the plant pot with flower 1¼" from top of A, lifting the top edge of the pot to place the stem underneath, referring to the overlap lines on the plant pot pattern and as shown in Figure 2.

6. Arrange the remaining stems, leaves and berry stems under the top edge of the plant pot as in step 5, referring to the overlap lines on the pot pattern and the Assembly Diagram; add remaining

flowers and the berries, again referring to patterns and Assembly Diagram. When satisfied with positioning, fuse shapes in place.

7. Using a machine- or hand-stitched buttonhole stitch and thread to match the background, machine-stitch around each shape to complete the appliquéd center.

Here's a Tip

A stabilizer may be used on the back side of A to prevent puckering during the machine-appliqué process. Most stabilizers are removed when the stitching is complete. It is available in wash-away, cut-away, tear-away and heat-away types. The choice of stabilizer depends on the fabric it will be used with. Check them out online and at your local quilt shop to learn more. You may want to experiment with a variety of types to find which stabilizer might work best for you.

Fall Splendor
Assembly Diagram 36" x 36"

Completing the Quilt

Refer to the Assembly Diagram for positioning of pieces for all steps.

1. Sew B strips to opposite sides and C strips to the top and bottom of the appliquéd center; press seams toward strips.

2. Join four D rectangles on the short ends to make a D strip; press. Repeat to make a total of four D strips. Sew a D strip to opposite sides of the appliquéd center; press seams toward the B strips. Sew an E square to each end of each remaining D strip; press. Sew these strips to the top and bottom of the appliquéd center; press seams toward the C strips.

3. Sew F strips to opposite sides and G strips to the top and bottom of the appliquéd center; press seams toward F and G strips.

4. Join five H rectangles on the short ends to make an H strip; press. Repeat to make a total of four H strips. Sew an H strip to opposite sides of the appliquéd center; press seams toward the F strips. Sew an I square to each end of each remaining H strip; press. Sew these strips to the top and bottom of the appliquéd center. Press seams toward the G strips.

5. Sew J strips to opposite sides and K strips to the top and bottom of the appliquéd center; press seams toward the J and K strips.

6. Join six L rectangles on the short ends to make an L strip; press. Trim ½" off each end to make a 2½" x 32½" strip. Repeat to make a total of four L strips. Sew an L strip to opposite sides of the appliquéd center; press seams toward the J strips. Sew an M square to each end of each remaining L strip; press. Sew these strips to the top and bottom of the appliquéd center to complete the pieced top; press seams toward the K strips.

7. Create a quilt sandwich referring to Finishing Your Quilt on page 48.

8. Quilt as desired.

9. Bind edges, referring to Finishing Your Quilt on page 48 to finish. ■

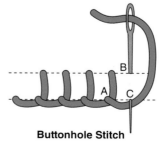

Buttonhole Stitch

"Fall is my favorite season. Days are warm, nights are cool, and colors are simply gorgeous! The colors of fall add so much warmth to a home—so, I guess I would have to say the season and its colors were my inspiration for this quilt." —Julie Weaver

Classic Elegance Bed Runner

Designed & Quilted by Julie Weaver

This project uses Courthouse Steps blocks in a stunning and versatile way—as a border that will impress. Grace your bed with quilted elegance.

Specifications
Skill Level: Confident Beginner
Bed Runner Size: 74" x 34"
Block Size: 8" x 8" finished
Number of Blocks: 22

Materials
- 6 fat quarters coordinating light cream/gray prints
- 6 fat quarters coordinating dark gray/cream prints
- ½ yard black-with-gray dots
- ½ yard cream/gray print
- 1⅛ yards black tonal
- Backing to size
- Batting to size
- Thread
- Basic sewing tools and supplies

Cutting

From each light cream/gray print:
- Cut 6 (1½" x 21") strips.
  Subcut strips into 44 each strips as follows:
  1½" x 2½" strip 1, 1½" x 4½" strip 3 and
  1½" x 6½" strip 5.

From each dark gray/cream print:
- Cut 8 (1½" x 21") strips.
  Subcut strips into 44 each strips as follows:
  1½" x 4½" strip 2, 1½" x 6½" strip 4 and
  1½" x 8½" strip 6.

From black-with-gray dots:
- Cut 2 (2½" by fabric width) strips.
  Subcut strips into 22 (2½") A squares.
- Cut 1 (8½" by fabric width) strip.
  Subcut strip into 2 (8½" x 16½") E rectangles.

From cream/gray print:
- Cut 1 (14½" by fabric width) strip.
  Trim strip to 1 (14½" x 38½") B rectangle.

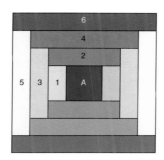

Courthouse Steps
8" x 8" Finished Block
Make 22

From black tonal:
- Cut 9 (1½" by fabric width) strips.
  Subcut strips into 2 each strips as follows:
  1½" x 14½" C, 1½" x 40½" D and 32½" F.
  Set aside remaining strips for G.
- Cut 6 (2¼" by fabric width) binding strips.

Completing the Courthouse Steps Blocks

1. Select one A square, two each light strips 1, 3 and 5 and two each dark strips 2, 4 and 6 to complete one Courthouse Steps block.

2. Sew a light strip 1 to opposite sides of A referring to Figure 1; press seams toward the strips.

Figure 1

Figure 2

3. Sew a dark strip 2 to the remaining sides of A to complete one round as shown in Figure 2; press seams toward the strips.

12

4. Continue adding strips to opposite sides of the stitched unit in numerical order to complete one Courthouse Steps block referring to Figure 3; press seams toward the strips just added.

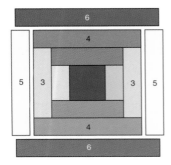

Figure 3

5. Repeat steps 1–4 to complete a total of 22 Courthouse Steps blocks.

Completing the Bed Runner

Refer to the Assembly Diagram for positioning of pieces and blocks for all steps.

1. Sew a C strip to opposite short ends and D strips to the long sides of B; press seams toward C and D strips.

Here's a Tip

Feature a beautiful print in the center, select a coordinating print, and then dig into your stash of scraps to find coordinating pieces from which to cut the strips for the Courthouse Steps blocks for this easy-to-stitch bed runner.

2. Sew an E rectangle to opposite short ends of the bordered B rectangle; press seams toward E.

3. Join two Courthouse Steps blocks on the dark edges to make an end row; press seam to one side. Repeat to make a second end row. Sew the end rows to opposite short ends of the bordered B rectangle; press seams toward the E rectangles.

4. Join nine Courthouse Steps blocks on the light edges to make a side row; press seams to one side. Repeat to make a second side row. Sew the side rows to opposite sides of the bordered B rectangle; press seams away from the side rows.

5. Sew F strips to opposite short ends of the bordered B rectangle; press seams toward F strips.

Classic Elegance Bed Runner
Assembly Diagram 74" x 34"

6. Join the G strips on the short ends to make a long strip; press. Subcut strip into two 1½" x 74½" G strips. Sew the strips to opposite long sides of the bordered B rectangle to complete the quilt top; press seams toward G strips.

7. Create a quilt sandwich referring to Finishing Your Quilt on page 48.

8. Quilt as desired.

9. Bind edges, referring to Finishing Your Quilt on page 48 to finish. ■

"I love, love, love this fabric. Grays and blacks are fast joining the ranks of new neutrals, and they combine for a very classy finished look. The Log Cabin block and its variations—in this case the Courthouse Steps variation—are so versatile and inspiring. One can change the look simply by turning the block." —Julie Weaver

Housing Boom

Designed & Quilted by Chris Malone

Create custom borders that echo the homes in your neighborhood. This runner will be the focal point on your table and the subject of many conversations.

Specifications

Skill Level: Confident Beginner
Table Runner Size: 48" x 18"
Block Sizes: 10" x 10" finished, 4" x 4" finished and 2" x 4" finished
Number of Blocks: 4, 24 and 10

Materials

- 42 (5") precut squares assorted colors including green
- 1 fat quarter red tonal
- ⅝ yard gray tonal
- 1 yard blue tonal
- Backing to size
- Batting to size
- Thread
- 1 yard fusible web
- Template material
- Basic sewing tools and supplies

Cutting

Prepare templates for appliqué shapes using patterns given on the pattern insert. Cut as directed and as per instructions. For variety, use blue or white 5" squares from a purchased charm pack or scraps to cut a few D squares to add variety to your piecing. See sample project photo for inspiration.

From red tonal:
- Cut 6 (2½" x 21") C strips.

From gray tonal:
- Cut 3 (2½" by fabric width) strips.
  Subcut strips into 6 (2½" x 21") A strips.
- Cut 4 (2¼" by fabric width) binding strips.

From blue tonal:
- Cut 4 (2½" by fabric width) strips.
  Subcut strips into 7 (2½" x 21") B strips.
- Cut 4 (4½" by fabric width) strips.
  Subcut strips into 20 (4½") D squares and 10 (2½" x 4½") E rectangles.

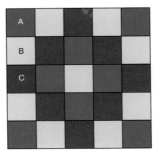

Building Blocks
10" x 10" Finished Block
Make 4

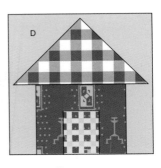

House
4 x 4 " Finished Block
Make 20

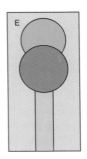

Double Tree
2" x 4" Finished Block
Make 4

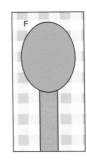

Oval Tree
2" x 4" Finished Block
Make 3

Single Tree
2" x 4" Finished Block
Make 3

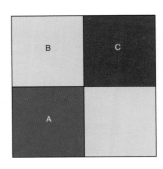

Four-Patch
4" x 4" Finished Block
Make 4

Completing the Building Blocks Blocks

1. Select one C strip and two each A and B strips. Sew an A strip to a B strip along length; repeat. Sew the C strip between the A-B strips to make an A-B-C-B-A strip set; press seams in one direction.

2. Subcut the strip set into eight (2½" x 10½") A-B-C-B-A units as shown in Figure 1.

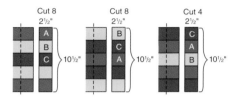

Figure 1

3. Select one A strip and two each B and C strips. Sew a B strip to a C strip along length; repeat. Sew the A strip between the B-C strips to make a B-C-A-C-B strip set; press seams in one direction.

4. Subcut the strip set into eight B-C-A-C-B units, again referring to Figure 1.

5. Select one B strip and two each A and C strips. Sew an A strip to a C strip along length; repeat. Sew a B strip between the A-C strips to make a C-A-B-A-C strip set; press seams in one direction.

6. Subcut the strip set into four C-A-B-A-C units, again referring to Figure 1.

7. To complete one Building Blocks block, select and join two each A-B-C-B-A and B-C-A-C-B units and one C-A-B-A-C unit referring to Figure 2; press seams in one direction. *Note: Turn strips as necessary to keep seams in adjoining units going in opposite directions when being stitched as shown in Figure 3.*

Figure 2   **Figure 3**

8. Repeat step 7 to complete a total of four blocks.

Completing the Four-Patch Blocks

1. Select one each A and B strip. Sew together with right sides together along length to make an A-B strip set; press seam toward A. Repeat with a B strip

and a C strip to make a B-C strip set; press seam toward C.

2. Subcut the A-B and B-C strip sets into four each 2½" x 4½" units as shown in Figure 4.

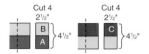

Figure 4

3. Select and join one each A-B and B-C unit to complete one Four-Patch block as shown in Figure 5; press seam to one side. Repeat to make a total of four blocks.

Figure 5

Completing the Appliquéd Blocks

1. Draw 20 (2½" x 2½") house squares, 20 (⅞" x 1¼") door rectangles and 10 (½" x 2¼") tree trunk rectangles on the paper side of the fusible web, leaving a small space between pieces when drawing.

2. Trace roof, oval and circle appliqué shapes given on the pattern insert onto the paper side of the fusible web referring to patterns for number to trace.

3. Cut out all fusible web shapes, leaving a margin around each one.

4. Divide 5" precut squares into house, tree and door fabrics referring to patterns and Assembly Diagram for color suggestions. Fuse cutout shapes to the wrong side of the chosen fabrics. Cut out shapes on traced lines; remove paper backing.

5. Select one D square and one each house, roof and door shape. Center the house shape on one edge of the D square and fuse in place referring to Figure 6.

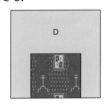

Figure 6   **Figure 7**

6. Center and fuse a door and roof shape on the house shape, overlapping the roof over the house enough to cover the raw edge referring to Figure 7.

7. Using thread to match fabrics and a narrow, close machine buttonhole stitch, sew around each appliqué shape to secure and complete one House block.

8. Repeat steps 5–7 to complete a total of 20 House blocks.

9. Select one E rectangle and one each Double 1 and Double 2 circle shape and tree trunk rectangle.

10. Center and fuse the tree trunk rectangle on the E rectangle as shown in Figure 8.

Figure 8

11. Center and fuse a Double 1 circle on the tree trunk and the Double 2 circle on top, overlapping as marked on pattern and referring to block drawing.

12. Stitch in place as in step 7 to complete one Double Tree block.

13. Repeat steps 9–12 to complete a total of four Double Tree blocks.

14. Repeat steps 9–12 with Oval and Single shapes to complete three each Oval Tree and Single Tree blocks.

Completing the Table Runner
Refer to the Assembly Diagram for positioning of all quilt components for all steps.

1. Arrange and join the four Building Blocks blocks to complete the pieced center; press seams to one side.

2. Join eight House blocks with two each Oval Tree and Double Tree blocks to make a side strip; press seams toward House blocks. Repeat with eight House blocks and one each Oval and Double Tree, and two Single Tree blocks to make a second side strip.

3. Sew side strips to opposite long sides of the pieced center; press seams away from the side strips.

4. Join two House blocks with a Double Tree block and add a Four-Patch block to each end to make an end strip; press seams away from the House blocks. Repeat with a Single Tree and two each House and Four-Patch blocks to make a second end strip.

5. Sew the end strips to opposite short ends of the pieced center to complete the pieced top; press seams away from the end strips.

6. Create a quilt sandwich referring to Finishing Your Quilt on page 48.

7. Quilt as desired.

8. Bind edges, referring to Finishing Your Quilt on page 48 to finish. ∎

"I think an interesting and colorful table runner is a great home decor piece. This one has a fairly simple patchwork center, where flowers, bread baskets, etc., can be placed without covering up the fun part of the design." —Chris Malone

Here's a Tip
Here are some tips for making accurate and straight strip sets.

- *Apply spray starch to the fabrics before cutting strips.*
- *Stitch with a smaller stitch length so seams won't come apart when pieces are cut from the strip.*
- *Before sewing, lay the strips on a flat surface to pin.*
- *Be careful not to pull on the top strip when feeding the strips through the machine.*
- *Before pressing the seams to one side, heat-set the stitches by pressing the seam in the closed position.*

Housing Boom
Assembly Diagram 48" x 18"

Hexie Festoon

Designed & Quilted by Maria Flora

Let the creative juices flow with your scraps and this pattern. A simple Nine-Patch and a fun, easy machine-appliquéd border are all you need to make a timeless treasure.

Specifications
Skill Level: Confident Beginner
Quilt Size: 41" x 53"
Block Size: 6" x 6" finished
Number of Blocks: 35

Materials
- ¼ yard total assorted white/green scraps for leaves
- ½ yard light print for binding
- 1½ yards total assorted bright scraps for Nine-Patch blocks, hexagons and yo-yos
- 2⅛ yards white solid
- Backing to size
- Batting to size
- Thread
- 7½ yards green jumbo rickrack
- Glue stick (optional for appliqué)
- Freezer paper (optional for hexagon appliqué)
- ½ yard fusible web (optional for leaf appliqué)
- Template material
- Basic sewing tools and supplies

Cutting
Prepare templates for appliqué pieces using patterns given on pattern insert. Cut pieces according to your favorite appliqué method referring to patterns for color and number to cut, adding a seam allowance to the leaf and hexagon pieces for turned-edge methods.

From light print:
- Cut 5 (2¼" by fabric width) binding strips.

From assorted bright scraps:
- Cut 18 sets of 5 same-fabric 2½" A squares.

From white solid:
- Cut 5 (2½" by fabric width) strips.
  Subcut strips into 72 (2½") B squares.
- Cut 3 (6½" by fabric width) strips.
  Subcut strips into 17 (6½") C squares.
- Cut 3 (6" by fabric width) D strips.
- Cut 2 (6" by fabric width) strips.
  Trim strips to make 2 (6" x 41½") E strips.

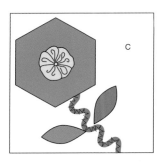

Hexie Flower
6" x 6" Finished Block
Make 17

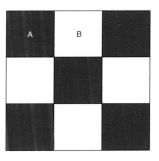

Nine-Patch
6" x 6" Finished Block
Make 18

Completing the Nine-Patch Blocks

1. Select one set of five same-fabric A squares and four B squares to complete one Nine-Patch block.

2. Sew a B square between two A squares to make the top row as shown in Figure 1; press seams toward A. Repeat to make the bottom row.

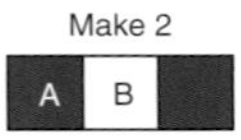

Make 2

Figure 1

3. Sew an A square between two B squares to make the center row as shown in Figure 2; press seams toward A.

Figure 2

4. Sew the center row between the top and bottom rows to complete one Nine-Patch block as shown in Figure 3; press seams in one direction.

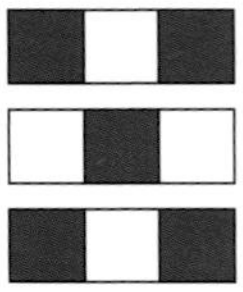

Figure 3

5. Repeat steps 1–4 to complete a total of 18 Nine-Patch blocks.

Preparing the Yo-Yo Flower Centers

1. Thread a needle and knot the end.

2. Working with the wrong side of the fabric toward you, turn under approximately ¼" of the edge of the circle.

3. Insert the needle in the edge of the fabric on the wrong side so the knot will be inside the yo-yo. Sew a basic running stitch around the edge of the circle, turning the edge under as you sew as shown in Figure 4. Stop when you reach starting point.

Figure 4

4. Hold the needle and thread, and pull the thread to gather the circle and tuck the turned edge into the center, keeping the right side of the fabric out as you gather to make an almost-closed circle as shown in Figure 5.

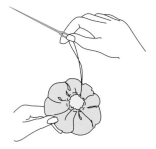

Figure 5

5. While holding, close to the fabric so the gathers do not slip, knot the thread multiple times; trim the thread close to the knots.

6. Using your hands, press the yo-yo flat with the hole in the center to finish as shown in Figure 6.

Figure 6

7. Repeat steps 1–6 to make a total of 35 yo-yos.

Here's a Tip

If this quilt will be used by a young child, simple fused circles may be used as flower centers instead of the yo-yos. If being used as a decorative wall quilt, buttons in a variety of sizes and colors may be substituted for the yo-yos as flower centers. Make this playful quilt your own by adding personal touches as desired.

Completing the Hexie Flower Blocks

1. Prepare the leaf and hexagon shapes for your favorite method of appliqué. ***Note:*** *See the Needle-Turn Appliqué sidebar on page 24 or the freezer-paper appliqué tips on page 23 for more appliqué choices. The leaf shapes are prepared for fusible appliqué.*

2. Select one C square, one prepared hexagon, two prepared leaves, one prepared yo-yo and the green jumbo rickrack.

3. Pin the hexagon anywhere on the C square, keeping the edges of the hexagon at least ½" from the edges of C as shown in Figure 7.

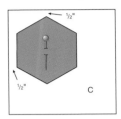

Figure 7

4. Pin or apply a few dabs of glue stick to the wrong side of the hexagon to temporarily hold in place.

5. Start a length of rickrack under the hexagon and end at any side of C, making curved or straight stems. When satisfied with rickrack angle and placement, pin or apply glue stick to hold in place and trim even with the edge of C referring to Figure 8.

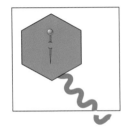

Figure 8

6. Arrange and apply two prepared leaf shapes using your favorite appliqué method.

7. Using thread to match the rickrack and a machine zigzag stitch, stitch through the center of the rickrack from one end to the other, lifting the hexagon out of the way when stitching the end that lies under the edge of the hexagon referring to Figure 9.

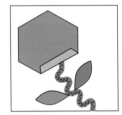

Figure 9

8. Stitch the hexagon in place by hand or machine as desired.

9. Center a prepared yo-yo in the hexagon and hand-stitch the edges in place referring to Figure 10 to complete one Hexie Flower block.

Figure 10

10. Repeat steps 2–9 to complete a total of 17 Hexie Flower blocks.

Completing the Quilt

Refer to the Placement Diagram for positioning of all quilt components for all steps.

1. Arrange and join three Nine-Patch blocks with two Hexie Flower blocks to make an X row; press seams toward Hexie Flower blocks. Repeat to make a total of four X rows.

2. Arrange and join three Hexie Flower blocks with two Nine-Patch blocks to make a Y row; press seams toward the Hexie Flower blocks. Repeat to make a total of three Y rows.

3. Join the X and Y rows to complete the quilt center; press seams in one direction.

4. Join the D strips on the short ends to make a long strip; press. Subcut strip into two 6" x 42½" D strips. Sew a D strip to opposite long sides of the quilt center; press seams toward the D strips.

5. Sew the E strips to the top and bottom of the quilt center; press seams toward the E strips.

6. Place prepared hexagons on the D and E strips aligned with the Nine-Patch blocks referring to Figure 11; pin or apply glue stick to hold in place.

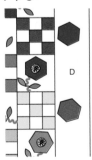

Figure 11

7. Center and secure a prepared hexagon in each corner.

8. Keeping the edge of the rickrack at least 1¼" from outer edge, run the rickrack from hexagon to hexagon, creating a smooth arc or festoon as you go; pin or apply glue stick to hold rickrack in place as you move from one hexagon to another. When satisfied with positioning, trim rickrack away from under hexagons, leaving just enough to tuck under the edges to be stitched in place.

9. Sew rickrack in place as in step 7 for Completing the Hexie Flower Blocks.

10. Stitch hexagons in place by hand or machine to complete the quilt top.

11. Create a quilt sandwich referring to Finishing Your Quilt on page 48.

12. Quilt as desired.

13. Bind edges, referring to Finishing Your Quilt on page 48 to finish. ■

"I love the look of appliqué but don't want to spend a lot of time on it. These easy hexie flowers with cheerful yo-yo centers and rickrack stems were the perfect alternate blocks for my scrap Nine-Patch blocks. The rickrack adds a lot of appeal without much work." —Maria Flora

Hexie Festoon
Placement Diagram 41" x 53"

Here's a Tip

Try freezer-paper appliqué for all types of shapes.

Trace the shapes onto the dull side of the freezer paper, tracing one for each piece needed (35 hexagons for this project); cut out shapes on traced lines.

Iron the freezer-paper shapes' shiny side to the wrong side of the fabrics; cut out shapes, leaving at least ⅛"–¼" extra all around for the turn-under seam allowance (Figure A).

Figure A

Dab water-soluble glue stick onto the edges of the freezer paper. Fold the seam allowance over the glue, one side at a time (Figure B).

Figure B

Finger-press edges flat.

Apply shapes to the background fabric using your favorite method.

Carefully cut a slit through the background fabric behind the shapes and trim to ¼" from stitching line (Figure C). Spray water on the back side of each appliqué shape.

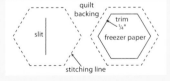

Figure C

Using tweezers, remove the freezer-paper shapes. Allow blocks to dry before joining with the Nine-Patch blocks.

Needle-Turn Appliqué

Hand appliqué takes more time than fusible appliqué, but for some people the results are worth the extra time and effort. Here are two popular methods for hand appliqué. Refer to your favorite complete quilting guide for more methods.

Freezer-Paper Appliqué

1. Trace around the finished pattern size (do not include seam allowance on the pattern) on the paper side of a sheet of freezer paper. Reverse the pattern for any directional shapes before tracing (Figure A). Trace the number of pieces needed to complete the project.

Figure A

2. Cut out the freezer-paper shapes on the traced lines. You can layer, pin and cut three or four layers at a time without sacrificing accuracy.

3. Place and press the freezer-paper shapes with the waxy/shiny side down on the wrong side of the fabric leaving ½" between pieces (Figure B). The freezer paper's waxy/shiny side will stick to the fabric when heated and can be reused several times.

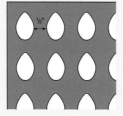

Figure B

4. Cut fabric pieces leaving a ¼" seam allowance beyond the edge of the freezer-paper shape (Figure C).

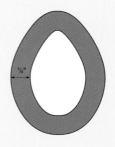

Figure C

5. Clip into curves almost to the paper shape (Figure D). Cut off sharp points ⅛"–¼" beyond the point of the freezer-paper pattern (Figure E). Clip into inside angles almost to the drawn line (Figure F).

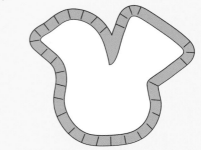

Figure D

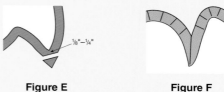

Figure E   **Figure F**

6. Fold edges over the freezer paper and iron in place a little section at a time (Figure G). This is easier to accomplish if using a mini iron.

Figure G

7. When edges are smooth, remove freezer paper (Figure H).

Figure H

8. Position the prepared shape on the background. Blind-stitch piece in place using thread to match the fabric by inserting a threaded needle into the folded edge and catching a few threads of the background before pulling out (Figure I). Stitches should not show.

Figure I

Turned-Edge Appliqué

1. Prepare a template for the appliqué shape without seam allowance, and trace around shape on the right side of the fabric using a fine-point pencil.

2. Cut out the shape ¼" beyond the marked line. Use thread to match the fabric to machine-stitch on the outside edge of the marked line (Figure J). Clip edges as shown in Figure D.

Figure J

3. Pin the cut shape in position on the background.

4. Turn in the fabric edge along the outer edge of the stitched line (Figure K). Blind-stitch the piece in place as you turn the edge in a little at a time (Figure L).

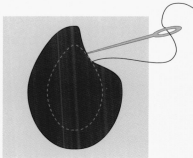

Figure K

Figure L

Here's a Few Tips

Some quilters use a dab of fabric glue stick to hold the seam allowance in place on the freezer paper. This makes it a little more difficult to remove the freezer paper, but it does make the edges stick down and gives a crisp edge to the shape.

Mylar template plastic may be used instead of freezer paper. The pieces may be used over and over again.

Spray sizing (not spray starch) is another alternative that provides a stiff edge for turning.

Checkerboard Beauty

Design by Nancy Scott
Quilted by Masterpiece Quilting

Build this border one step at a time and make a simple quilt pop. A checkerboard with a triple-pieced mitered border on both sides is the perfect way to make a quilt larger without sacrificing design.

Specifications
Skill Level: Intermediate
Quilt Size: 60" x 72"
Block Sizes: 12" x 12" finished and 4" x 4" finished
Number of Blocks: 12 and 54

Materials
- 2 yards aqua tonal
- 2⅜ yards white solid
- 3¼ yards navy tonal
- Backing to size
- Batting to size
- Thread
- Basic sewing tools and supplies

Cutting

From aqua tonal:
- Cut 10 (3⅞" by fabric width) strips.
  Subcut strips into 96 (3⅞") A squares.
- Cut 7 (2½" by fabric width) D strips.

From white solid:
- Cut 4 (3⅞"-wide) strips along the length of the fabric.
  Subcut strips into 72 (3⅞") C squares.
- Cut 8 (1½"-wide) strips along the length of the fabric for F, G, H and I borders.

From navy tonal:
- Cut 3 (3⅞" by fabric width) strips.
  Subcut strips into 24 (3⅞") B squares.
- Cut 7 (2½" by fabric width) E strips.
- Cut 16 (2"-wide) strips along the remaining length of the fabric for F, G, H and I borders.
- Cut 4 (2¼"-wide) binding strips along the remaining length of fabric.

Completing the Checkerboard Blocks
1. Mark a diagonal line from corner to corner on the wrong side of each A square.

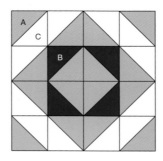

Checkerboard
12" x 12" Finished Block
Make 12

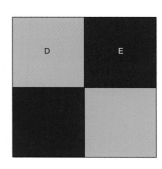

Four-Patch
4" x 4" Finished Block
Make 54

2. Referring to Figure 1, place an A square right sides together with a B square and stitch ¼" on each side of the marked line. Cut apart on the marked line and press open to make two A-B units as shown in Figure 1. Repeat to make a total of 48 A-B units.

Figure 1

3. Repeat step 2 with A and C squares to make 144 A-C units referring to Figure 2; press.

Figure 2

4. Arrange and join four A-C units to make the top row as shown in Figure 3; press. Repeat to make the bottom row.

Figure 3

5. Arrange and join two A-C units with two A-B units to make a center row as shown in Figure 4; press. Repeat to make a second center row.

Make 2

Figure 4

6. Arrange and join the rows referring to Figure 5 to complete one Checkerboard block; press.

Figure 5

Mitered Corner Borders

1. Add at least twice the border width to the border lengths measured or instructed to cut.

2. Center and sew the side borders to the quilt, beginning and ending stitching ¼" from the quilt corner and backstitching (Figure A). Repeat with the top and bottom borders.

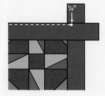

¼"

Figure A

3. Fold and pin quilt right sides together at a 45-degree angle on one corner (Figure B). Place a straightedge along the fold and lightly mark a line across the border ends.

Figure B

4. Stitch along the line, backstitching to secure. Trim seam to ¼" and press open (Figure C).

¼"

Figure C

7. Repeat steps 4–6 to complete a total of 12 Checkerboard blocks.

Completing the Four-Patch Blocks

1. Sew a D strip to an E strip along the length to make a D-E strip set; press. Repeat to make a total of seven D-E strip sets.

2. Subcut the D-E strip sets into 108 (2½" x 4½") D-E segments as shown in Figure 6.

Cut 108
2½"

D
E } 4½"

Figure 6

3. To complete one Four-Patch block, join two D-E segments as shown in Figure 7; press. Repeat to make a total of 54 Four-Patch blocks.

Figure 7

Checkerboard Beauty
Assembly Diagram 60" x 72"

Completing the Quilt

1. Arrange and join three Checkerboard blocks to make a row; press. Repeat to make a total of four rows.

2. Join the rows and press to complete the pieced center; press.

3. Sew a 1½"-wide white border strip between two 2"-wide navy border strips along length to make a navy/white/navy border strip; press. Repeat with remaining strips to make a total of eight navy/white/navy border strips.

4. Trim the navy/white/navy border strips into two each border strips as follows: 4½" x 62" F, 4½" x 50" G, 4½" x 78" H and 4½" x 66" I.

5. Center and sew an F strip to opposite long sides and G strips to the top and bottom of the quilt center, stopping stitching ¼" from corners and mitering corners referring to Mitered Corner Borders on page 28; press.

6. Join 14 Four-Patch blocks to make a side block strip referring to the Assembly Diagram; press. Repeat to make a second side block strip. Sew these strips to opposite long sides of the bordered quilt center; press.

7. Repeat step 6 with 13 Four-Patch blocks to make the top strip; press. Repeat to make the bottom strip. Sew these strips to the top and bottom of the bordered quilt center; press.

8. Center and sew the H strips to opposite long sides and I strips to the top and bottom of the quilt center, stopping stitching ¼" from corners and mitering corners referring to Mitered Corner Borders on page 28, to complete the quilt top; press.

9. Create a quilt sandwich referring to Finishing Your Quilt on page 48.

10. Quilt as desired.

11. Bind edges, referring to Finishing Your Quilt on page 48 to finish. ■

"In what is becoming my style, very traditional quilt features, including the pieced blocks and thin mitered borders, gain a trendy look with updated colors." —Nancy Scott

Blushing Stars

Designed & Quilted by Lolita Newman of Stitchin' By The River Studio

This pieced border complements the center blocks and makes a spectacular finish. This project would look lovely in almost any fabrics.

Specifications
Skill Level: Intermediate
Quilt Size: 52½" x 52½"
Block Size: 12" x 12" finished
Number of Blocks: 5

Materials
- 1¼ yards cream solid
- 1½ yards tangerine tonal
- 2¼ yards black print
- Backing to size
- Batting to size
- Thread
- Basic sewing tools and supplies

Cutting

From cream solid:
- Cut 1 (3⅞" by fabric width) strip.
  Subcut strip into 8 (3⅞") squares. Cut each square in half on 1 diagonal to make 16 B triangles.
- Cut 1 (4¼" by fabric width) strip.
  Subcut strip into 8 (4¼") squares. Cut each square on both diagonals to make 32 C triangles.
- Cut 1 (2⅜" by fabric width) strip.
  Subcut strip into 16 (2⅜") squares. Cut each square in half on 1 diagonal to make 32 D triangles.
- Cut 2 (3½" by fabric width) strips.
  Subcut strips into 16 (3½") G squares.
- Cut 1 (4⅞" by fabric width) strip.
  Subcut strip into 3 (4⅞") H squares and 2 (3⅜") O squares. Cut the H squares in half on 1 diagonal to make 6 H triangles and the O squares on both diagonals to make 8 O triangles.
- Cut 1 (2⅞" by fabric width) strip.
  Subcut strip into 10 (2⅞") squares. Cut each square in half on 1 diagonal to make 20 J triangles.
- Cut 2 (5⅜" by fabric width) strips.
  Subcut strips into 10 (5⅜") U squares and 4 (2") P squares. Cut the U squares on both diagonals to make 40 U triangles.

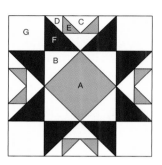

Blushing Star
12" x 12" Finished Block
Make 4

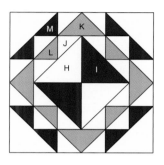

Center
12" x 12" Finished Block
Make 1

From tangerine tonal:
- Cut 1 (4¾" by fabric width) strip.
  Subcut strip into 4 (4¾") A squares.
- Cut 1 (2⅜" by fabric width) strip.
  Subcut strip into 16 (2⅜") squares. Cut each square in half on 1 diagonal to make 32 E triangles.
- Cut 1 (18¼" by fabric width) strip.
  Subcut strip into 1 (18¼") Q square, 1 (5¼") K square, 2 (2⅞") L squares and 4 (4⅝") Y squares. Cut the Q and K squares on both diagonals to make 4 each Q and K triangles. Cut the L squares in half on 1 diagonal to make 4 L triangles.
- Cut 2 (9½" by fabric width) strips.
  Subcut strips into 5 (9½") X squares and 2 (9⅜") R squares. Cut each X square on both diagonals to make 20 X triangles and each R square in half on 1 diagonal to make 4 R triangles.

From black print:
- Cut 2 (3⅞" by fabric width) strips.
  Subcut strips into 16 (3⅞") squares. Cut each square in half on 1 diagonal to make 32 F triangles.
- Cut 1 (5⅜" by fabric width) strip.
  Subcut strip into 2 (5⅜") V squares, 1 (4⅞") I square and 4 (2⅞") M squares. Cut each V square in half on both diagonals to make 8 V triangles. Cut each I and M square in half on 1 diagonal to make 2 I triangles and 8 M triangles.

- Cut 1 (12½" by fabric width) strip.
  Subcut strip into 16 (2" x 12½") N strips.
- Cut 9 (2" by fabric width) S/T/Z/ZZ border strips.
  Trim 2 strips to 2" x 38¾" for S strips.
  Trim 2 strips to 2" x 41¾" for T strips.
  Set aside remaining strips for Z/ZZ strips.
- Cut 2 (3⅜" by fabric width) strips.
  Subcut strips into 16 (3⅜") W squares.
- Cut 6 (2¼" by fabric width) binding strips.

Completing the Center Block

1. Select two I triangles, four each K and L triangles, six H triangles, eight M triangles and 20 J triangles to complete the Center block.

2. Sew J to each side of L to make a J-L unit as shown in Figure 1; press seams away from L. Repeat to make a total of four J-L units.

Make 4

Figure 1

3. Sew an H triangle to a J-L unit to make an H-J-L unit as shown in Figure 2; press seam toward H. Repeat to make a second H-J-L unit.

Make 2

Figure 2

4. Repeat step 3 with I triangles and the remaining J-L units to make two I-J-L units as shown in Figure 3; press seams toward I.

Make 2

Figure 3

5. Referring to Figure 4, join one each H-J-L and I-J-L unit to make a row; repeat to make a second row. Press seams toward the I-J-L units. Join the rows to complete the block center; press.

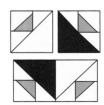

Figure 4

6. Sew J to each short side of K and add M to complete a side unit as shown in Figure 5; press seams away from K and toward M. Repeat to make a total of four side units.

Make 4

Figure 5

7. Sew a side unit to opposite sides of the block center and add H triangles to each corner to complete the Center block referring to Figure 6; press seams open and then toward H.

Figure 6

Completing the Blushing Star Blocks

1. Select one A square, four B triangles, four G squares and eight each C, D, E and F triangles to complete one Blushing Star block.

2. Sew B to each side of A to complete the center unit as shown in Figure 7; press seams toward B.

Make 4

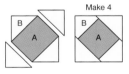

Figure 7

3. Sew E to each short side of C and add D and then C triangles to make a triangle unit as shown in Figure 8; press seams toward E, D and then C. Repeat to make a total of four triangle units.

Make 4

Figure 8

4. Sew an F triangle to each triangle unit to make side units referring to Figure 9; press seams toward F.

Make 4

Figure 9

5. Sew a side unit to opposite sides of the center unit to make the center row as shown in Figure 10; press seams toward the center unit.

Figure 10

6. Sew a G square to each end of each remaining side unit to make the top row as shown in Figure 11; press seams toward G. Repeat to make the bottom row.

Make 2

Figure 11

7. Sew the top and bottom rows to the center row to complete one Blushing Star block as shown in Figure 12; press seams open.

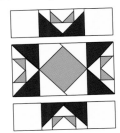

Figure 12

8. Repeat steps 1–7 to complete a total of four Blushing Star blocks.

Completing the Side Border Strips

1. Sew a U triangle to two adjacent sides of a W square to make a U-W unit as shown in Figure 13; press seams toward W. Repeat to make a total of 16 U-W units.

Make 16

Figure 13

2. Sew a U triangle to a V triangle on the short sides to make an end unit as shown in Figure 14; press seam toward V. Repeat to make a reverse end unit, again referring to Figure 14. Repeat to make a total of four each end and reverse end units.

Figure 14

3. Select and join four U-W units with five X triangles and one each end and reverse end unit to make a side border strip referring to Figure 15; press seams toward X. Repeat to make a total of four side border strips.

Make 4

Figure 15

Completing the Quilt

Refer to the Assembly Diagram for positioning of the quilt components for all steps.

1. Arrange and join three N strips with two each O triangles and P squares to make a long sashing strip; press seams toward N. Repeat to make a second long sashing strip.

2. Sew an O triangle to opposite ends of an N strip to make a short sashing strip; press seams toward N. Repeat to make a second short sashing strip.

3. Join two Blushing Star blocks with the Center block, four N strips and two R triangles to make the center block row; press seams toward N.

4. Sew an N strip to opposite sides of a Blushing Star block and add a Q triangle to each N side to complete a short block row; press seams toward N. Repeat to make a second short block row.

5. Sew R to a short sashing strip to make a corner unit; press seam toward R. Repeat to make a second corner unit.

6. Join the long block row with long sashing strips, and then add the two short block rows and the corner units to complete the quilt center; press seams away from the block rows.

7. Sew S strips to the top and bottom, and T strips to opposite sides of the quilt center; press seams toward S and T.

8. Sew a side border strip to opposite sides of the quilt center; press seams toward T strips.

9. Sew a Y square to each end of each remaining side border strip; press seams toward Y. Sew these strips to the top and bottom of the quilt center; press seams toward S strips.

10. Join the Z/ZZ strips on the short ends to make a long strip; press. Subcut strip into two 2" x 50" Z strips and 2" x 53" ZZ strips.

11. Sew Z strips to the top and bottom, and ZZ strips to opposite sides of the quilt center to complete the quilt top; press seams toward Z and ZZ strips.

12. Create a quilt sandwich referring to Finishing Your Quilt on page 48.

13. Quilt as desired, being careful not to stitch though the C units.

14. Bind edges, referring to Finishing Your Quilt on page 48 to finish. ■

Blushing Stars
Assembly Diagram 52 1/2" x 52 1/2"

"I tend to let the blocks dictate what will happen in my quilts."
—Lolita Newman

Blue Moon

Design by Lyn Brown
Quilted by Cindy Kruse

This quick and easy quilt becomes fabulous when a faux bargello border is added.
This technique produces a border that would look great on almost any quilt.

Specifications

Skill Level: Confident Beginner
Quilt Size: 88" x 88"
Block Sizes: 20" x 20" finished, 10" x 10" finished
  and 12" x 12" finished
Number of Blocks: 9, 24 and 4

Materials

- 45 (2½" x 42") A precut strips dark blue batiks
- ⅜ yard each 4 different dark blue batiks
- ⅞ yard dark blue dotted batik
- 1¼ yards each 5 different white/blue batiks
- Backing to size
- Batting to size
- Thread
- Basic sewing tools and supplies

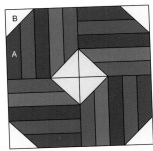

Blue Moon
20" x 20" Finished Block
Make 9

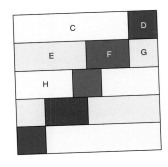

Border
10" x 10" Finished Block
Make 24

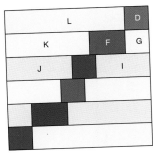

Corner
12" x 12" Finished Block
Make 4

Cutting

From 4 dark blue batiks:
- Cut 9 assorted 2½" by fabric width strips.
  Subcut 1 strip from each fabric into 4 (2½")
  D squares and 2 (2½" x 3½") F rectangles.
  Set aside 5 remaining strips for D strip sets.
- Cut 3 assorted 3½" by fabric width F strips.

From dark blue dotted batik:
- Cut 9 (2¼" by fabric width) binding strips.

From white/blue batiks:
- Cut 3 assorted 2½" by fabric width G strips.
- Cut 6 assorted 2½" by fabric width strips.
  Subcut strips into 8 strips each 2½" x 5" I,
  2½" x 6" J, 2½" x 7½" K and 2½" x 10½" L.
- Cut 4 assorted 4½" by fabric width H strips.
- Cut 3 assorted 5½" by fabric width E strips.
- Cut 3 assorted 8½" by fabric width C strips.
- Cut 8 assorted 4½" by fabric width strips.
  Subcut strips into 72 (4½") B squares.
- Cut 16 assorted 2½" by fabric width strips.
  Subcut strips into 4 (2½" x 12½") M strips,
  4 (2½" x 14½") N strips, 24 (2½" x 20½")
  O strips and 8 (2½") G squares.

Completing the Blue Moon Blocks

1. Select five random A strips and join with right sides together along length to make an A strip set; press. Repeat to make nine A strip sets.

2. Subcut A strip sets into 36 (10½" x 10½") A units referring to Figure 1.

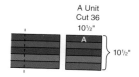

A Unit
Cut 36
10½"

10½"

Figure 1

3. Mark a diagonal line from corner to corner on the wrong side of each B square.

4. Place a B square right sides together on opposite corners of an A unit and stitch on the marked lines referring to Figure 2.

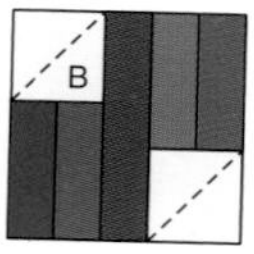

B

B

Figure 2

5. Trim seam allowance to ¼" and press B to the right side to complete one A-B unit as shown in Figure 3.

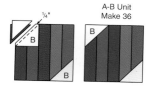

¼"

A-B Unit
Make 36

B

B

B

Figure 3

6. Repeat steps 4 and 5 with remaining A units and B squares to make a total of 36 A-B units.

7. Select four A-B units. Join two units to make a row; repeat to make a second row. Press seams to one side. Join the rows to complete one Blue Moon block as shown in Figure 4; press.

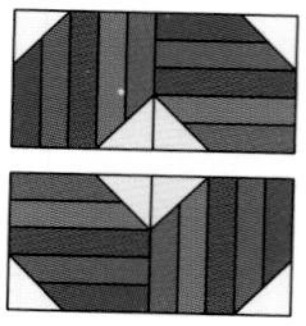

Figure 4

8. Repeat step 7 to make a total of nine Blue Moon blocks.

Completing the Border Blocks

1. Sew a C strip to a D strip with right sides together along length to make a C-D strip set; press seam toward D. Repeat to make a total of three C-D strip sets.

2. Sew an F strip between a G strip and an E strip as in step 1 to make a total of three E-F-G strip sets.

3. Subcut the C-D and E-F-G strip sets into 48 (2½" x 10½") units each as shown in Figure 5.

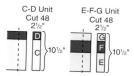

C-D Unit
Cut 48
2½"

E-F-G Unit
Cut 48
2½"

D

C

10½"

G

F

E

10½"

Figure 5

4. Sew a D strip between two H strips as in step 1 to make a total of two D-H strip sets. Subcut strip sets into 24 (2½" x 10½") D-H units as shown in Figure 6.

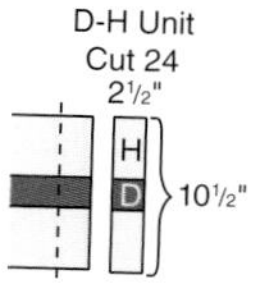

D-H Unit
Cut 24
2½"

H

D

10½"

Figure 6

5. Select one D-H unit and two each C-D and E-F-G units to complete one Border block.

6. Arrange and join the units as shown in Figure 7 to complete one Border block; press seams to one side.

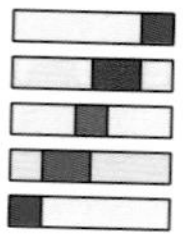

Figure 7

7. Repeat steps 5 and 6 to make a total of 24 Border blocks.

Completing the Corner Blocks

1. Select two F rectangles, two G squares, four D squares, and two each I, J, K and L rectangles to complete one Corner block.

2. Referring to Figure 8, sew D to L to complete a D-L row; press seam toward D. Repeat to make a second D-L row.

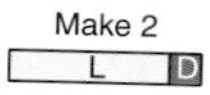

Make 2

Figure 8

3. Sew F between G and K to make a G-F-K row as shown in Figure 9; press seams toward F. Repeat to make a second G-F-K row.

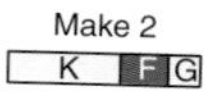

Make 2

Figure 9

4. Sew D between I and J to make an I-D-J row as shown in Figure 10; press seams toward D. Repeat to make a second I-D-J row.

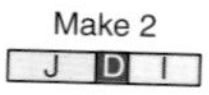

Make 2

Figure 10

5. Arrange and join the rows as shown in Figure 11 to make one Corner block; press.

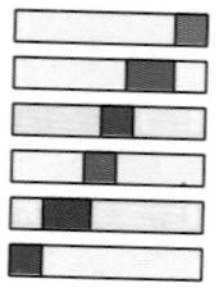

Figure 11

6. Repeat steps 1–5 to make a total of four Corner blocks.

Completing the Quilt

1. Sew an M strip to one side and an N strip to an adjacent side of each Corner block to make four corner units as shown in Figure 12; press seams toward M and N strips.

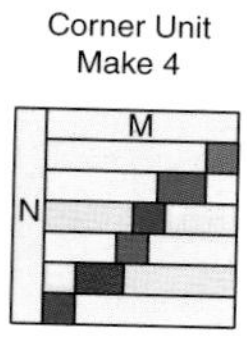

Corner Unit
Make 4

Figure 12

2. Join two Border blocks and add an O strip to each long side to make a side border unit as shown in Figure 13; press seams toward O strips. Repeat to make a total of 12 side border units.

Side Unit
Make 12

Figure 13

3. Arrange and join the Blue Moon blocks in three rows of three blocks each referring to the Assembly Diagram; press.

4. Join three side border units to make a side border strip; press. Repeat to make a total of four side border strips. Sew a side border strip to opposite sides of the quilt center; press seams toward the strips.

5. Sew a corner unit to each end of each remaining side border strip; press. Sew these strips to the top and bottom of the quilt center to complete the quilt top; press.

6. Create a quilt sandwich referring to Finishing Your Quilt on page 48.

7. Quilt as desired.

8. Bind edges, referring to Finishing Your Quilt on page 48 to finish. ∎

*"I am a big fan of the Rail Fence block. It is
so easy to make, and with the packets of
2½" precut strips, it's even easier! I wondered
how the block could be changed and found
that adding triangles to two corners of the
units before joining into blocks made a
dramatic difference."* —Lyn Brown

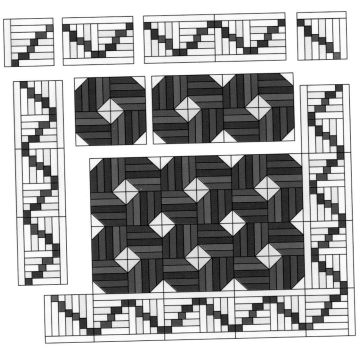

Blue Moon
Assembly Diagram 88" x 88"

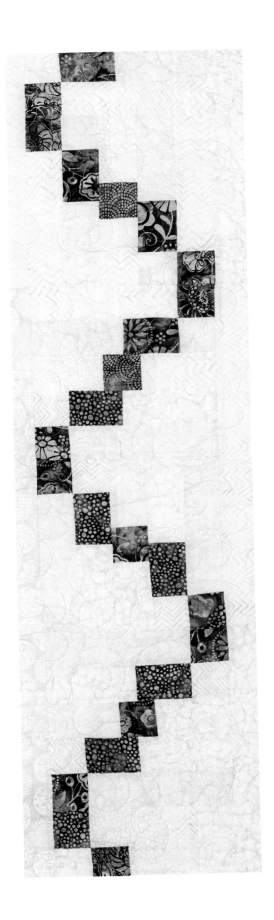

Border Rhythm

Design by Jenny Rekeweg
Quilted by Masterpiece Quilting

Bring rhythm to your quilt with the "beats" of random piecing. Create a unique border that will be the focus of this quilt in colors of your choice.

Specifications
Skill Level: Confident Beginner
Quilt Size: 60" x 60"
Block Size: 8" x 8" finished
Number of Blocks: 9

Materials
- ⅝ yard rust solid chambray
- ⅔ yard purple solid chambray
- 4½ yards gold solid chambray
- Backing to size
- Batting to size
- Thread
- Basic sewing tools and supplies

Cutting

From rust solid chambray:
- Cut 7 (2¼" by fabric width) binding strips.

From purple solid chambray:
- Cut 10 (1¾" by fabric width) B strips.

From gold solid chambray:
- Cut 10 (3¼" by fabric width) A strips.

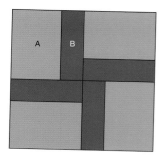

Rhythm
8" x 8" Finished Block
Make 9

- Cut 8 (4½" by fabric width) strips.
  Subcut strips into rectangles as follows:
  5 (4½" x 8½") C, 16 (4½" x 6") D, 11 (4½" x 3½") E and 11 (4½" x 8") F.
- Cut the remaining fabric into strips of random widths from 2½" to 10" by fabric width for framing the blocks.

Completing the Rhythm Blocks
1. Sew an A strip to a B strip with right sides together along length to make an A-B strip set; press seam toward B. Repeat to make 10 A-B strip sets.

2. Subcut four of the A-B strip sets into 36 (4½" x 4½") A-B units as shown in Figure 1; set aside remaining strip sets for border sections.

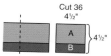

Cut 36
4½"

A
B
4½"

Figure 1

3. Select four A-B units. Join two units to make a row referring to Figure 2; repeat to make a second row. Press seams toward the B side.

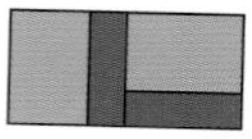

Make 2

Figure 2

Here's a Tip
The chambray fabrics used in this quilt are woven with different-color horizontal and vertical threads. This fabric reads different colors when placed in different directions. This adds visual movement to the quilt. Depending on which direction the fabrics are placed, different shades appear.

4. Join the rows as shown in Figure 3 to make one Rhythm block; press.

Figure 3

5. Repeat steps 3 and 4 to make a total of nine Rhythm blocks.

Framing the Blocks

1. Select one Rhythm block and several random-width gold solid strips.

2. In a crazy-patchwork or Log-Cabin fashion, sew a strip to a block; open and press seam toward the strip and then trim the strip even with the block as shown in Figure 4.

Figure 4

Free-Form Piecing

Free-form piecing is fun. While you may be playful when creating the framed blocks, they do have to conform to a size when joined to make rows to complete the quilt center.

Although the framed blocks finish to a variety of sizes, the goal for this quilt center is to measure 44½" (including seam allowance) when finished in order for it to work with the pieced borders.

This is accomplished by joining three framed blocks to make a vertical row. Then the center vertical row is trimmed to 16½" x 44½". Repeat with the remaining two rows and trim to 14½" x 44½" to complete the side rows. Even though the framing strips are random widths, you have to conform to a size at some point, even in this free-form method.

3. Continue adding strips to each side of the block, pressing and trimming after each addition, to frame the block on all sides with random-width strips as shown in Figure 5. **Note:** *Three framed blocks must measure at least 16½" wide for blocks in the center row and the remaining six blocks must measure at least 14½" wide for each of the two side rows. See Free-Form Piecing for more information.*

Figure 5

4. Repeat all steps with the remaining blocks referring to the Assembly Diagram for possible layouts.

5. Join three blocks to make a row; press seams to one side. Repeat to make a total of three rows.

6. Trim the center row to 16½" x 44½" and each side row to 14½" x 44½".

Completing the Border Strips

1. Subcut the remaining A-B strip sets into the following size segments referring to Figure 6: 16 (3" x 4½") A-B2, 11 (5½" x 4½") A-B3, 11 (1" x 4½") A-B4 and nine 8½" x 4½" A-B5.

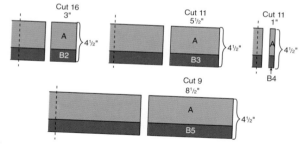

Figure 6

2. Sew an A-B2 segment to D to make a D unit as shown in Figure 7; press seam toward D. Repeat to make a total of 16 D units.

Figure 7   **Figure 8**

3. Sew an A-B3 segment to E to make an E unit as shown in Figure 8; press seam toward E. Repeat to make a total of 11 E units.

4. Sew an A-B4 segment to F to make an F unit as shown in Figure 9; press seam toward F. Repeat to make a total of 11 F units.

F Unit
Make 11

F

A → ← B4

Figure 9

Completing the Quilt

1. Join the completed and trimmed rows to complete the quilt center referring to the Assembly Diagram; press.

2. Arrange and join the pieced border units with the A-B5 segments and the C rectangles to make one each 11-unit and 15-unit strip, and two 13-unit strips, referring to the Assembly Diagram; press.

3. Sew the 11-unit strip to the bottom of the quilt center; press.

4. Sew a 13-unit strip to the left side and then the remaining 13-unit strip to the top of the quilt center; sew the 15-unit strip to the remaining side to complete the quilt top. Press.

5. Create a quilt sandwich referring to Finishing Your Quilt on page 48.

6. Quilt as desired.

7. Bind edges, referring to Finishing Your Quilt on page 48 to finish. ∎

The idea of this quilt came to me while listening to John Mayer's first CD, Inside Wants Out. The idea of a stereo's base line came to mind … and I chose to illustrate that base line circling around the body of the quilt." —Jenny Rekeweg

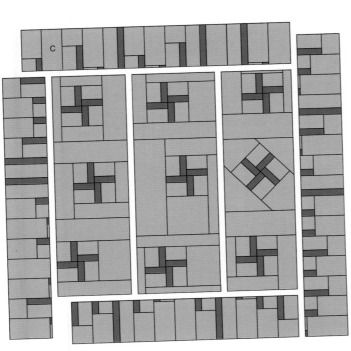

Border Rhythm
Assembly Diagram 60" x 60"

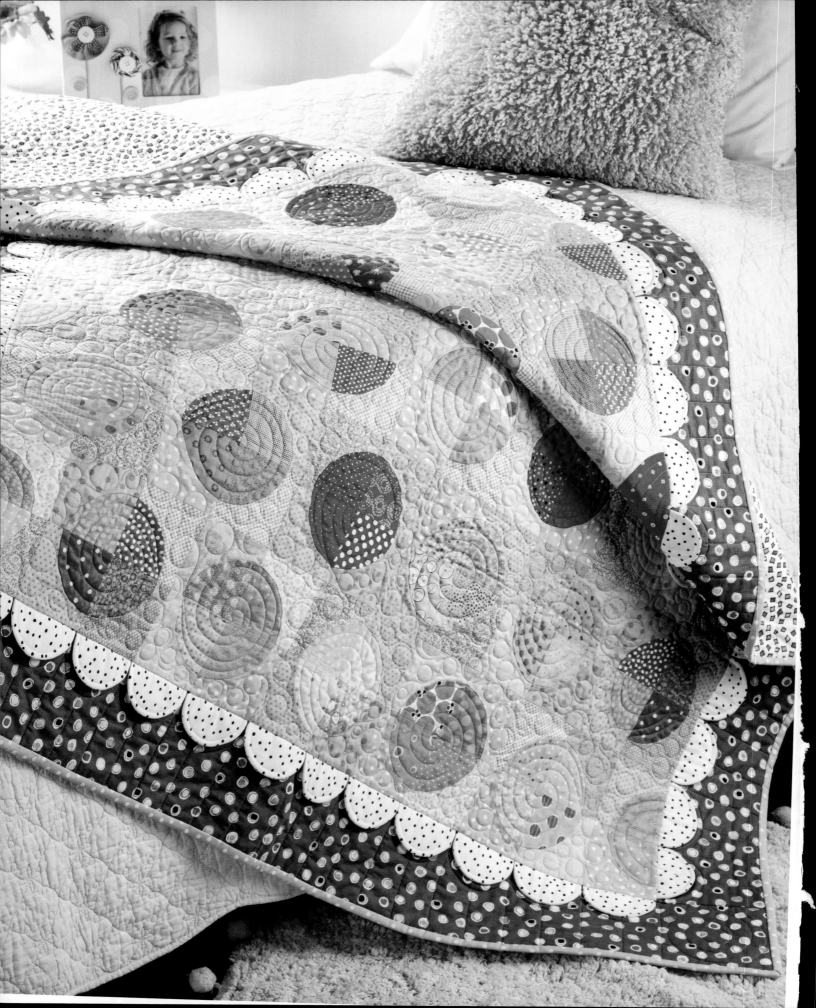

Lotsa Dots

Design by Chris Malone
Quilted by Jean McDaniel

Strategic block placement of Drunkard's Path blocks to create dots and then bringing half dots out to the border in a lovely and clever 3-D border accent makes a stunning baby or lap quilt.

Specifications
Skill Level: Intermediate
Quilt Size: 52" x 66"
Block Sizes: 7" x 7" finished, 3½" x 7" finished
Number of Blocks: 44 and 8

Materials
- ⅝ yard light gray-with-white dots
- 1 yard white-with-black dots
- 1⅛ yards dark gray dot print
- 1¾ yards total assorted dots, prints and/or tonals in yellow, green, orange, red, pink, purple and blue
- 2¾ yards total assorted light gray dots, prints and/or tonals
- Backing to size
- Batting to size plus 3 (5" x 21") rectangles
- Thread
- Template material
- Pinking shears
- Basic sewing tools and supplies

Cutting
Prepare templates for A, B and C pieces using patterns given on pattern insert. Cut as directed on patterns and instructions.

From light gray-with-white dots:
- Cut 6 (2¼" by fabric width) binding strips.

From white-with-black dots:
- Cut 7 (4" by fabric width) C strips.

From dark gray dot print:
- Cut 6 (5½" by fabric width) D/E strips.

Completing the Blocks
1. Select one set of four same-color–family B pieces and four A pieces. Fold each A and B piece in half and crease to mark the center as shown in Figure 1.

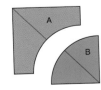

Figure 1

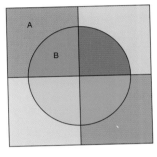

Drunkard's Path
7" x 7" Finished Block
Make 44

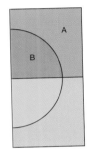

Half Drunkard's Path
3½" x 7" Finished Block
Make 8

2. Center and sew a B piece to an A piece to complete an A-B unit referring to Figure 2; press seam toward B. Repeat to make a total of four A-B units.

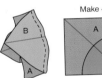

Make 4

Figure 2

3. Arrange and join the four A-B units in two rows of two units each as shown in Figure 3; press seams open. Join the rows to complete one Drunkard's Path block; press seams open.

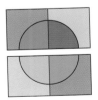

Figure 3

4. Repeat steps 1–3 to complete a total of 44 Drunkard's Path blocks.

5. Repeat steps 1–3 using just two same-color–family B pieces and two A pieces to make one stitched row to complete each of the eight Half Drunkard's Path blocks referring to Figure 4.

Figure 4

Preparing the C Units

1. Trace four sets of two C pieces onto the wrong side of half of one C strip, tracing one C against another C, sharing the same straight-edge cutting line and leaving ½" between the pairs as shown in Figure 5.

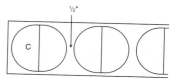

Figure 5

2. Fold the marked C strip in half with right sides together and pin on top of a batting rectangle as shown in Figure 6.

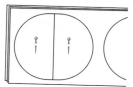

Figure 6

3. Repeat steps 1 and 2 to trace 56 C pieces.

4. Stitch on the traced curved lines through all layers of each marked C strip as shown in Figure 7.

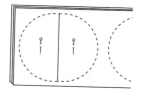

Figure 7

5. Cut apart on the marked straight lines. Using pinking shears, cut close to, but not touching, the stitched curved edges as shown in Figure 8.

Figure 8

6. Turn trimmed C units right side out and press edges smooth. Topstitch ⅝" from the curved edge and machine-baste ⅛" in from the open edge of each unit closed as shown in Figure 9 to complete the units. Press again after stitching.

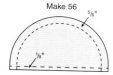

Make 56

⅝"

⅛"

Figure 9

Completing the Quilt

Refer to the Assembly Diagram for positioning of all quilt components for all steps.

1. Arrange and join six Drunkard's Path blocks to make an X row; press seams open. Repeat to make a total of four X rows.

2. Arrange and join five Drunkard's Path blocks with two Half Drunkard's Path blocks to make a Y row; press seams open. Repeat to make a total of four Y rows.

3. Arrange and join the X and Y rows to complete the quilt center; press seams open.

4. Join the D/E strips on the short ends to make a long strip; press. Subcut strip into two each 5½" x 56½" D strips and 5½" x 52½" E strips.

5. Arrange, pin and baste 16 C units on one long edge of each D strip beginning ¼" from each end, and 12 C units on one long edge of each E strip beginning 5¼" from each end, referring to Figure 10 and the Assembly Diagram.

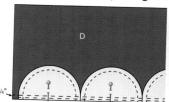

Figure 10

6. Sew a D strip to opposite sides and E strips to the top and bottom of the quilt center; press seams away from the D and E strips.

7. Create a quilt sandwich referring to Finishing Your Quilt on page 48.

8. Quilt as desired, being careful not to stitch though the C units.

9. Bind referring to Finishing Your Quilt on page 48 to finish. ■

"I love dots and bright colors—both seem uplifting and happy. I also love adding a little dimension, as in the border scallops." —Chris Malone

Here's a Few Tips

Try these few time-saving tips.

• *Look for Drunkard's Path acrylic templates, which are available in your local quilt shop or online, to use for cutting with a rotary cutter.*

• *When using a pattern repeatedly, as in the scallops in this project, try cutting the template out of coarse sandpaper. It won't slip on the fabric and will last for many tracings.*

• *Pair A and B pieces and have them handy whenever you have a few minutes to pin; then place them by your sewing machine.*

• *Chain-stitch the seams and you will find that you can get a lot accomplished with even small amounts of time.*

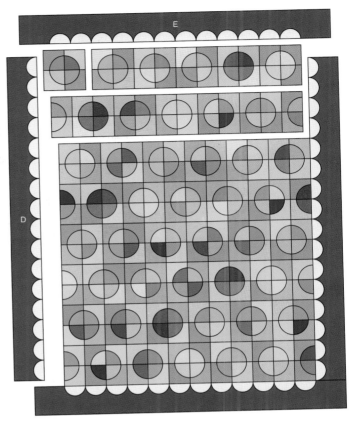

Lotsa Dots
Assembly Diagram 52" x 66"

Finishing Your Quilt

1. Press quilt top on both sides; check for proper seam pressing and trim all loose threads.

2. Sandwich batting between the stitched top and the prepared backing piece; pin or baste layers together to hold. Mark quilting design and quilt as desired by hand or machine.

3. When quilting is complete, remove pins or basting. Trim batting and backing fabric edges even with raw edges of quilt top.

4. Join binding strips on short ends with diagonal seams to make one long strip; trim seams to ¼" and press seams open.

5. Fold the binding strip in half with wrong sides together along length; press.

6. Sew binding to quilt edges, matching raw edges, mitering corners and overlapping ends.

7. Fold binding to the back side and stitch in place to finish.

Special Thanks

Please join us in thanking the talented designers whose work is featured in this collection.

Lyn Brown
Blue Moon, page 35

Maria Flora
Hexie Festoon, page 19

Chris Malone
Housing Boom, page 14
Lotsa Dots, page 45

Lolita Newman
Blushing Stars, page 31

Jenny Rekeweg
Border Rhythm, page 40

Nancy Scott
Checkerboard Beauty, page 26

Julie Weaver
Classic Elegance Bed Runner, page 11
Fall Splendor, page 6

Supplies

We would like to thank the following manufacturers who provided materials to our designers to make sample projects for this book.

Fall Splendor, page 6: Warm & Natural cotton batting and Lite Steam-A-Seam 2 Double Stick fusible web from The Warm Company.

Classic Elegance Bed Runner, page 11: Little Black Dress 2 fabric collection from Moda; Warm & Natural cotton batting from The Warm Company.

Housing Boom, page 14: Flats fabric collection by Angela Yosten for Moda.

Checkerboard Beauty, page 26: Digital quilting patterns from TK Quilting & Design LLC.

Blue Moon, page 35: Pacific BaliPops and Frost Batiks from Hoffman California Fabrics.

Border Rhythm, page 40: Carolina Chambrays.

Annie's

Quilts With Unique Borders is published by Annie's, 306 East Parr Road, Berne, IN 46711. Printed in USA. Copyright © 2014 Annie's. All rights reserved. This publication may not be reproduced in part or in whole without written permission from the publisher.

RETAIL STORES: If you would like to carry this pattern book or any other Annie's publication, visit AnniesWSL.com.

Every effort has been made to ensure that the instructions in this pattern book are complete and accurate. We cannot, however, take responsibility for human error, typographical mistakes or variations in individual work. Please visit AnniesCustomerCare.com to check for pattern updates.

ISBN: 978-1-57367-456-0
23456789